ALSO BY M. SCOTT PECK, M.D.

THE ROAD LESS TRAVELED
*A New Psychology of Love, Traditional Values
and Spiritual Growth*

PEOPLE OF THE LIE
The Hope for Healing Human Evil

WHAT RETURN CAN I MAKE?
Dimensions of the Christian Experience
(with Marilyn von Waldner and Patricia Kay)

THE DIFFERENT DRUM
Community-Making and Peace

A BED BY THE WINDOW
A Novel of Mystery and Redemption

THE FRIENDLY SNOWFLAKE
A Fable of Love, Faith and Family
(illustrated by Christopher Scott Peck)

A WORLD WAITING TO BE BORN
Rediscovering Civility

A   TOUCHSTONE   BOOK

Published by Simon & Schuster
New York London Toronto Sydney Tokyo Singapore

MEDITATIONS

f r o m

THE ROAD

Daily Reflections from
The Road Less Traveled
and *The Different Drum*

M. SCOTT PECK M.D.

TOUCHSTONE
Simon & Schuster Building
1230 Avenue of the Americas
New York, New York 10020

TOUCHSTONE and colophon are registered
trademarks of Simon & Schuster Inc.

Designed by Bonni Leon-Berman
Manufactured in the United States of America

1 3 5 7 9 10 8 6 4 2

Library of Congress Cataloging-in-Publication Data
is available.

ISBN 0-671-79799-9

INTRODUCTION

Perhaps the most often quoted sentence from *The Road Less Traveled* is the one that opens the book: "Life is difficult." On an intellectual level, this might be translated as "There are no easy answers." Nor will you find easy answers in this book, which consists of other excerpts taken from both *The Road Less Traveled* and *The Different Drum**. My lectures are often hour-long elaborations of just one or two of these brief quotations. Even then I warn my audiences, "There is an exception to everything I am going to say today." Therefore, please do not regard these excerpts as quick, complete solutions. Rather they are more complex and sometimes perplexing messages, insights, ideas, and perceptions that require further reflection.

*All page references are to the regular trade paperback editions.

With this sole caveat, I believe you will find this book to be of value in your life and in the lives of your friends and families. In fact, one of its major purposes is to encourage you to think deeply—meaning, mostly, to think for yourself. While there is no doubt in my mind that my writings have benefited from grace (including the grace of good editors), they are not the word of God. Don't hesitate to be critical or skeptical in thinking about them. Indeed, a number of them emphasize the necessity of skepticism as a prerequisite for clear thinking. For instance, in *The Different Drum*, I address the subject of integrity in thinking, and the quote from it for November 27 advises, "If you wish to discern either the presence or absence of integrity, you need to ask only one question. What is missing? Has anything been left out?" I urge you to ask these same questions on every page of this book.

I have presented these excerpts in the form of daily meditations. In the two books from which they were taken, they appear in the contexts of my practice as a psychiatrist and as an observer of human behavior, my experiences as both a leader and a member of diverse groups working to achieve true community, and, above all, my own journey toward spirituality. Such precepts cannot, of course, be completely divorced from the case studies and particular situations that inspired them. And with each one, I have indicated where it can be found in *The Road Less Traveled* and *The Different Drum*. Thus, this book can be used as both a companion and a guide if you wish to explore them further as they initially evolved. Here, however, it is my intention, and my hope, that these quotations will find their context, and their

9

meaning, in the individual lives and experiences of all who read and contemplate them.

When we consider all the angles in our contemplation of ourselves and our lives, we find ourselves thinking holistically or paradoxically. Consequently, you will find much paradox in these pages. Do not be dismayed by this. Rather, you should rejoice in it. Revel in it. I am reminded of the renowned professor of philosophy who had a student who inquired one day, "Sir, it is said you believe that at the core of all truth there resides paradox. Is that correct?" "Well, yes and no," the great professor replied.

One common form of prayer of meditation is to contemplate a single, written excerpt for a period of time. In the Judeo-Christian tradition the excerpt is usually a Bible verse. In Buddhism, it is likely a brief word puzzle or koan. But it can be a poem or a part of a poem or anything that deserves attention deeper than a passing glance. That is the way this book is intended to be used. Its quotations are not for skimming. They are meant for meditation in silence and solitude. Go deeper with them. Grow with them. Go deeper into their wisdom and your own. Go deeper into the paradox.

Let me give you a recent example of this process in action within a group setting. I was participating in the leadership of a three-day conference on "Community, Spirituality, and Discipline." By the end of the first day, it had become clear to me that most of the participants were unusually sophisticated people, possessing (or possessed by) graduate degrees in psychology, theology, education, or business. On the second morning, from long experience, I told them that it is easier for unsophisticated people to achieve real community than sophisticated ones. To reach community, people must "empty" themselves of their titles and credentials and academic detachment. Already I had emphasized that community building was a spiritual discipline akin to prayer. "You don't have to throw away all your knowledge," I explained, "but you need to make room for something more." I requested them as a group of over one hundred souls to sit silently in their auditorium seats together for ten minutes while contemplating a single, simple sentence. Then in front of them I unveiled a flip chart on which, in large letters, were written the words of another and greater author: "Ye must be as wise as serpents and innocent as doves."

Please join us in this dynamic, contemplative work.

Once we truly know that life is difficult—once we truly understand and accept it—then life is no longer difficult. Because once it is accepted, it no longer matters.

RLT, p. 15

Life is a series of problems. Do we want to moan about them or solve them?

RLT, p. 15

Without discipline we can solve nothing. With only some discipline we can solve only some problems. With total discipline we can solve all problems.

RLT, p. 15–16

Problems are the cutting edge that distinguishes between success and failure. Problems call forth our courage and our wisdom; indeed, they create our courage and our wisdom.

RLT, p. 16

Wise people learn not to dread but actually to welcome problems because it is in this whole process of meeting and solving problems that life has its meaning.

RLT, p. 16

The tools of discipline are techniques by which we experience the pain of problems in such a way as to work them through and solve them successfully, learning and growing in the process. When we teach ourselves discipline, we are teaching ourselves how to suffer and also how to grow.

RLT, p. 17–18

Y ou can enhance the pleasure of life by meeting and experiencing the pain first and getting it over with.

RLT, p. 19

The time and the quality of the time that their parents devote to them indicate to children the degree to which they are valued by their parents.

RLT, p. 23

When children know that they are valued, when they truly feel valued in the deepest parts of themselves, then they feel valuable. This knowledge is worth more than any gold.

RLT, p. 24

The feeling of being valuable is a cornerstone of self-discipline because when you consider yourself valuable you will take care of yourself—including things like using your time well. In this way, self-discipline is self-caring.

RLT, p. 24

You can solve any problem if you are simply willing to take the time.

RLT, p. 28

Problems do not go away. They must be worked through or else they remain, forever a barrier to the growth and development of the spirit.

RLT, p. 30

We cannot solve life's problems except by solving them.

RLT, p. 32

We must accept responsibility for a problem before we can solve it. We cannot solve a problem by saying "It's not my problem," and hoping that someone else will solve it for us. We can solve a problem only when we say "This is *my* problem and it's up to me to solve it."

RLT, p. 32

To be free people we must assume total responsibility for ourselves, but in doing so we must possess the capacity to reject responsibility that is not truly ours.

RLT, p. 64

The problem of distinguishing what we are and what we are not responsible for is one of the greatest problems of human existence. To perform this process adequately we must possess the willingness and the capacity to suffer continual self-examination.

RLT, p. 37

It is only through a vast amount of experience and a lengthy and successful maturation that we gain the capacity to see the world and our place in it realistically, and thus are enabled to realistically assess our responsibility for ourselves and the world.

RLT, p. 37

No problem can be solved until an individual assumes the responsibility for solving it.

RLT, p. 39

By attempting to avoid the responsibility for our own behavior, we are giving away our power to some other individual or organization. In this way, millions daily attempt to escape from freedom.

RLT, p. 42

As adults, our choices are almost unlimited, but that does not mean they are not painful. Frequently our choices lie between the lesser of two evils, but it is still within our power to make these choices.

RLT, p. 42–43

The entirety of one's adult life is a series of personal choices, decisions. If we can accept this totally, then we become free people. To the extent that we do not accept this we will forever feel ourselves victims.

RLT, p. 44

If our lives are to be healthy and our spirits are to grow, we must be dedicated to the truth. For truth is reality. And the more clearly we see the reality of the world, the better equipped we are to deal with the world.

RLT, p. 44

Our view of reality is like a map with which to negotiate the terrain of life. If the map is false and inaccurate, we generally will be lost. If the map is true and accurate, we will generally know where we are, and if we have decided where we want to go, we will generally know how to get there.

RLT, p. 44

Only a relative and fortunate few continue until the moment of death exploring the mystery of reality, revising their maps of it, ever enlarging and refining and redefining their understanding of the world and what is true.

RLT, p. 45

The biggest problem of making internal maps of reality is not that we have to start from scratch, but that if our maps are to be accurate we have to continually revise them.

RLT, p. 45

We must always hold truth, as best we can determine it, to be more important, more vital to our self-interest, than our comfort.

RLT, p. 50

What does a life of total dedication to the truth mean? It means a life of continuous and never-ending stringent self-examination.

RLT, p. 51

The life of wisdom must be
a life of contemplation combined
with action.

RLT, p. 51

To know the world, we must not only examine it but we must simultaneously examine the examiner.

RLT, p. 51

Fortunately, we are beginning to realize that the sources of danger to the world lie more within us than outside, and that the process of constant self-examination and contemplation is essential for ultimate survival.

RLT, p. 51–52

Examination of the world without is never as personally painful as examination of the world within.

RLT, p. 52

A life of total dedication to the truth also means a life of willingness to be personally challenged. Accepting and even welcoming challenges to our maps of reality allow us to grow in wisdom and effectiveness.

RLT, p. 52–53

Perhaps the characteristic that makes us most human is our capacity to do the unnatural, to transcend and hence transform our own nature.

RLT, p. 53

Our ordinary interactions—at the water cooler, in conference, on the golf course, at the dinner table, in bed when the lights are out—offer us daily opportunities to risk the openness that leads to growth and happiness.

RLT, p. 54

The healing of the spirit has not been completed until open-ness to challenge becomes a way of life.

RLT, p. 54

The reason people lie is to avoid the pain of challenge and its consequences.

RLT, p. 55

The act of withholding the truth is always potentially a lie.

RLT, p. 62

The rewards of the difficult life of honesty and dedication to the truth are continual growth, effective intimate relationships, and the knowledge that one has served as a source of illumination and clarification to the world.

RLT, p. 63

By their openness, people dedicated to the truth live in the open, and through the exercise of their courage to live in the open, they become free from fear.

RLT, p. 63

Courageous people must continually push themselves to be completely honest, yet must also possess the capacity to withhold the whole truth when appropriate.

RLT, p. 64

To be organized and efficient, to live wisely, we must daily delay gratification and keep an eye on the future; yet to live joyously we must also possess the capacity, when it is not destructive, to live in the present and act spontaneously.

RLT, p. 64

The act of giving something up is painful. But as we negotiate the curves and corners of our lives, we must continually give up parts of ourselves. The only alternative is not to travel at all on the journey of life.

RLT, p. 66–67

To function successfully in our complex world it is necessary for us to possess the capacity not only to express our anger but also not to express it.

RLT, p. 65

We not only need to know how to deal with our anger in different ways at different times but also how most appropriately to match the right time with the right style of expression.

RLT, p. 65

What makes transition periods like the "mid-life crisis" problematic and painful is that in successfully working our way through them we must give up cherished notions and old ways of doing and looking at things.

RLT, p. 71

When we cling, often forever, to our old patterns of thinking and behaving, we fail to negotiate any crisis, to truly grow up, and to experience the joyful sense of rebirth that accompanies the successful transition into greater maturity.

RLT, p. 71

It is in the giving up of self that human beings can find the most ecstatic and lasting, solid, durable joy of life.

RLT, p. 72

It is death that provides life with all its meaning.

RLT, p. 72

The farther one travels on the journey of life, the more births one will experience, and therefore the more deaths—the more joy and the more pain. But for all that is given up even more is gained.

RLT, p. 73–74

Once suffering is completely accepted, it ceases in a sense to be suffering.

RLT, p. 75

The unceasing practice of discipline leads to mastery.

RLT, p. 75

The spiritually evolved individual is an extraordinarily loving individual, and with his or her extraordinary love comes extraordinary joy.

RLT, p. 75

Spiritually evolved people, by virtue of their discipline, mastery and love, are people of great power, although the world may generally behold them as quite ordinary people, since more often than not they will exercise their power in quiet or even hidden ways.

RLT, p. 75

One measure—and perhaps the best measure—of a person's greatness is the capacity for suffering. Yet the great are also joyful. This, then, is the paradox.

RLT, p. 76

The best decision-makers are those who are willing to suffer the most over their decisions but still retain their ability to be decisive.

RLT, p. 76

Buddha and Christ were not all that different. The suffering of Christ letting go on the cross and the joy of Buddha letting go under the bo tree are one.

RLT, p. 76

If your goal is to avoid pain and escape suffering, I would not advise you to seek higher levels of consciousness or spiritual evolution.

RLT, p. 76

You must forge for yourself
an identity before you can give it
up.

RLT, p. 76

Discipline is the means of human spiritual evolution. But what provides the motive, the energy for discipline? This force I believe to be love.

RLT, p. 81

I define love thus: The will to extend one's self for the purpose of nurturing one's own or another's spiritual growth.

RLT, p. 81

The act of loving is an act of self-evolution even when the purpose of the act is someone else's growth.

RLT, p. 82

We are incapable of loving another unless we love ourselves.

RLT, p. 82

We cannot forsake self-discipline and at the same time be disciplined in our care for another.

RLT, p. 83

We cannot be a source of strength unless we nurture our own strength.

RLT, p. 83

Not only do self-love and love of others go hand in hand but ultimately they are indistinguishable.

RLT, p. 83

One extends one's limits
only by exceeding them.

RLT, p. 83

Love is not effortless. It becomes demonstrable or real only through the fact that for that some-one (or for ourself) we take an extra step or walk an extra mile.

RLT, p. 83

Love is an act of will—
namely, both an intention and an
action. Love is as love does.

RLT, p. 83

Of all the misconceptions about love the most powerful and pervasive is the belief that "falling in love" is love. But it does lead us to make commitments from which real love may begin and gives us a foretaste of the more lasting mystical ecstasy that can be ours after a lifetime of love.

RLT, p. 84–97

Real love often occurs in a context in which the feeling of love is lacking, when we act lovingly despite the fact that we don't feel loving.

RLT, p. 88

We can choose how to respond to the experience of falling in love, but we cannot choose the experience itself.

RLT, p. 89

Real love is a permanently self-enlarging experience.

RLT, p. 89

True acceptance of their own and each other's individuality and separateness is the only foundation upon which a mature marriage can be based and real love can grow.

RLT, p. 93

The path to sainthood goes through adulthood. There are no quick and easy shortcuts.

RLT, p. 97

One must find one's self
before one can lose it.

RLT, p. 97

Lasting enlightenment or true spiritual growth can be achieved only through the persistent exercise of real love.

RLT, p. 97

Love is the free exercise of choice. Two people love each other only when they are quite capable of living without each other but *choose* to live with each other.

RLT, p. 98

The only way to be assured of being loved is to be a person worthy of love.

RLT, p. 102

The only true end of love is spiritual growth or human evolution.

RLT, p. 106

Saints must sleep and even prophets must play.

RLT, p. 107

Love is not simply giving;
it is *judicious* giving and judicious
withholding as well.

RLT, p. 111

Fostering independence is more loving than taking care of people who could otherwise take care of themselves.

RLT, p. 113

The paradox of love is that it is both selfish and unselfish at the same time.

RLT, p. 116

Genuine love implies commitment and the exercise of wisdom.

RLT, p. 117–118

Couples sooner or later always fall out of love, and it is at the moment when the mating instinct has run its course that the opportunity for genuine love begins.

RLT, p. 118

The person who truly loves does so because of a decision to love. This person has made a commitment to be loving whether or not the loving feeling is present.

RLT, p. 119

It is easy and not at all unpleasant to find evidence of love in one's feelings. It may be difficult and painful to search for evidence of love in one's actions.

RLT, p. 119

If an act is not one of work or courage, then it is not an act of love.

RLT, p. 120

By far the most important form of attention we can give our loved ones is listening.

RLT, p. 129

True listening is love in action.

RLT, p. 128

People handle their fear of change in different ways, but the fear is inescapable if we are in fact to change.

RLT, p. 131

Courage is not the absence of fear; it is the making of action in spite of fear.

RLT, p. 131

On some level spiritual growth, and therefore love, always requires courage and involves risk.

RLT, p. 131

If you are determined not to risk pain, then you must do without many things: having children, getting married, the ecstasy of sex, the hope of ambition, friendship—all that makes life alive, meaningful and significant.

RLT, p. 133

Grow in any dimension and pain as well as joy will be your reward. The only alternative is not to live fully or not to live at all.

RLT, p. 133

If we can live with the knowledge that death is our constant companion, then death can become our "ally," still fearsome but continually a source of wise counsel.

RLT, p. 133

When we shy away from death, the ever-changing nature of things, we inevitably shy away from life.

RLT, p. 134

All life itself represents a risk, and the more lovingly we live our lives the more risks we take.

RLT, p. 134

Of the thousands, maybe even millions, of risks we can take in a lifetime the greatest is the risk of growing up.

RLT, p. 134

Growing up is the act of taking a fearful leap into the unknown, undetermined, unsafe, insecure, unsanctified, and unpredictable. It is a leap that many people never really take in their lifetimes.

RLT, p. 134–136

The only real security in
life lies in relishing life's insecurity.

RLT, p. 136

It is only when one has taken the leap into the unknown of total selfhood, psychological independence and unique individuality that one is free to proceed along still higher paths of spiritual growth and free to manifest love in its greatest dimensions.

RLT, p. 139

Commitment is the foundation, the bedrock of any genuinely loving relationship.

RLT, p. 140

Deep commitment does not guarantee the success of the relationship but does help more than any other factor to assure it.

RLT, p. 140

It is our sense of commitment after the wedding which makes possible the transition from falling in love to genuine love. And it is our commitment after conception which transforms us from biological into psychological parents.

RLT, p. 140

It is impossible to truly understand another without making room for that person within yourself.

RLT, p. 149

To respond to our children's needs we must change ourselves. Only when we are willing to undergo the suffering of such changing can we become the parents our children need us to be.

RLT, p. 149

Learning from their children is the best opportunity most people have to assure themselves of a meaningful old age.

RLT, p. 150

Possibly the greatest risk of
love is the risk of exercising power
with humility.

RLT, p. 150

Genuine love recognizes and respects the unique individuality and separate identity of the other person.

RLT, p. 151

No marriage can be judged truly successful unless husband and wife are each other's best critics.

RLT, p. 153

Mutual loving confrontation is a significant part of all successful and meaningful human relationships. Without it the relationship is either unsuccessful or shallow.

RLT, p. 153

If we want to be heard we must speak in a language the listener can understand and on a level at which the listener is capable of operating.

RLT, p. 154

Only out of the humility
of love can humans dare to be God.

RLT, p. 155

Self-discipline is usually
love translated into action.

RLT, p. 155

Our feelings are the source of our energy; they provide the horsepower that makes it possible for us to accomplish the tasks of living.

RLT, p. 156

Since our feelings work for us, we should treat them with respect.

RLT, p. 156

Because genuine love involves an extension of oneself, vast amounts of energy are required. So, like it or not, we simply cannot love everyone.

RLT, p. 157

Genuine love is precious, and those who are capable of genuine love know that their loving must be focused as productively as possible through self-discipline.

RLT, p. 158

If you can say that you have built genuinely loving relationships with a spouse and children, then you have already succeeded in accomplishing more than most people accomplish in a lifetime.

RLT, p. 159

Freedom and discipline are indeed handmaidens; without the discipline of genuine love, freedom is invariably nonloving and destructive.

RLT, p. 159

Genuine love is self-replenishing. The more you nurture the spiritual growth of others, the more your own spiritual growth is nurtured.

RLT, p. 160

As I grow through love,
so grows my joy, ever more present,
ever more constant.

RLT, p. 160

The genuine lover always respects and even encourages separateness and the unique individuality of the beloved.

RLT, p. 160

Marriage is a truly co-operative institution, requiring great mutual contributions of care, time and energy, but existing for the primary purpose of nurturing each of the participants for individual journeys toward his or her own individual peaks of spiritual growth.

RLT, p. 167

Male and female both must tend the hearth [of a marriage] and both must venture forth.

RLT, p. 167

It is the separateness of the partners that enriches the union.

RLT, p. 168

Genuine love not only respects the individuality of the other but actually seeks to cultivate it, even at the risk of separation or loss.

RLT, p. 168

Significant journeys cannot be accomplished without the nurture provided by a successful marriage or a successful society.

RLT, p. 168

It is the return of the individual to the nurturing marriage or society from the peaks he or she has traveled alone which serves to elevate that marriage or that society to new heights.

RLT, p. 168

While we in the West seem to be embarrassed by the subject of love, Hindu gurus make no bones about the fact that their love is the source of their power.

RLT, p. 173

Any genuinely loving relationship is one of mutual psychotherapy.

RLT, p. 178

All human interactions
are opportunities either to learn or
to teach.

RLT, p. 179

When my beloved first stands before me naked, all open to my sight, there is a feeling throughout the whole of me; awe. Why? If sex is no more than an instinct, why don't I simply feel horny or hungry? Such simple hunger would be quite sufficient to insure the propagation of the species. Why awe? Why should sex be complicated by reverence?

RLT, p. 181

As we grow in discipline, love and life experience, our understanding of the world and our place in it naturally grows apace. This understanding is our religion.

RLT, p. 185

We tend to believe what the people around us believe and to accept as truth what they tell us of the nature of reality.

RLT, p. 189

It is not so much what our parents say that determines our world view as it is the unique world they create for us by their behavior.

RLT, p. 189

The path to holiness lies through questioning *everything*.

RLT, p. 194

To be the best of which we are capable, our religion [or world view] must be a wholly personal one, forged entirely through the fire of our questioning and doubting in the crucible of our own experience of reality.

RLT, p. 194

We cannot consider our-
selves to know something unless we
have actually experienced it.

RLT, p. 195

It is essential to our spiritual growth for us to become scientists who are skeptical of the common notions and assumptions of our culture. But the notions of science themselves often become cultural idols, and it is necessary that we become skeptical of these as well.

RLT, p. 223

It is indeed possible for us to mature out of a belief in God. What I would now like to suggest is that it is also possible to mature into a belief in God.

RLT, p. 223

The God that comes before skepticism may bear little resemblance to the God that comes after.

RLT, p. 224

When we are able to say that "a human is both mortal and eternal at the same time" and "light is both a wave and a particle at the same time," science and religion have begun to speak the same language, that of paradox.

RLT, p. 227

We have been looking for the burning bush, the parting of the sea, the bellowing voice from heaven. Instead we should be looking at the ordinary day-to-day events in our lives for evidence of the miraculous.

RLT, p. 230

Just as it is essential that our sight not be crippled by scientific tunnel vision, so also is it essential that our critical faculties and capacity for skepticism not be blinded by the brilliant beauty of the spiritual realm.

RLT, p. 232

There is a force, the mechanics of which we do not fully understand, that seems to operate routinely in most people to protect and to foster their mental and physical health even under the most adverse conditions. The religious have applied to it the name of grace.

RLT, p. 237–260

If you work long and hard enough to understand yourself, you will come to discover that your unconscious, a vast part of your mind of which you now have little awareness, contains riches beyond imagination.

RLT, p. 243

The messages our unconscious gives us through dreams always seem to be designed to nurture our spiritual growth—as warnings of personal pitfalls; as guides to the solution of problems; as encouragement that we are right when we think we are probably wrong; and as direction-finders when we feel lost.

RLT, p. 245

The unconscious may communicate to us when we are awake with as much elegance and beneficence as when we are asleep. These "idle thoughts" usually provide us with dramatic insight into ourselves.

RLT, p. 245

The problem is not that human beings have hostile and sexual feelings, but rather that human beings have a conscious mind that is so often unwilling to face these feelings and tolerate the pain of dealing with them, and that is so willing to sweep them under the rug.

RLT, p. 248

We are almost always either less or more competent than we believe ourselves to be. The unconscious, however, knows who we really are.

RLT, p. 251

The fact of the matter is that our unconscious is wiser than we are about everything.

RLT, p. 251

All knowledge and all wisdom seem to be contained in our minds, and when we learn "something new" we are actually only discovering something that existed in our self all along.

RLT, p. 252

The mind, which some-times presumes to believe that there is no such thing as a miracle, is it-self a miracle.

RLT, p. 253

Grace is available to everyone, but while some take advantage of it, others do not.

RLT, p. 257

Touched by grace, highly unlikely beneficial events happen to us all the time, quietly, knocking on the door of our awareness no more dramatically than the beetle gently tapping on the windowpane.

RLT, p. 259

I do not think we can hope to approach a full understanding of the cosmos, or of the place of man within the cosmos, without incorporating the phenomenon of grace into our conceptual framework. To do so seems perilous.

RLT, p. 261

Our lifetime offers us unlimited opportunities for spiritual growth until the end.

RLT, p. 263

Given what we understand of the universe, evolution should not exist at all. The most striking feature of the process is that it is a miracle.

RLT, p. 263

There is a force that somehow pushes us to choose the more difficult path whereby we can transcend the mire and muck into which we are so often born. Despite all that resists the process, we do become better human beings.

RLT, p. 266

Those who achieve growth not only enjoy the fruits of growth but give the same fruits to the world.

RLT, p. 267

Evolving as individuals,
we carry humanity on our backs.
And so humanity evolves.

RLT, p. 267

What is this force that pushes us as individuals and as a whole species to grow against the natural resistance of our own lethargy? It is love.

RLT, p. 268

It is through love that we elevate ourselves. And it is through our love for others that we assist others to elevate themselves.

RLT, p. 268

The evolutionary force, present in all of life, manifests itself in mankind as human love.

RLT, p. 268

If we take it seriously, we are going to find that the simple notion of a loving God does not make for an easy philosophy.

RLT, p. 269

Why does God want us to grow? What is it that God wants of us?

RLT, p. 269

All of us who postulate a loving God and really think about it eventually come to a single terrifying idea: God wants us to become Himself (or Herself or Itself).

RLT, p. 269–270

It is God who is the source
of the evolutionary force and God
who is the destination.

RLT, p. 270

It is one thing to believe in a nice old God who will take good care of us from a lofty position of power. It is quite another to believe in a God who has it in mind for us that we should attain His position, His power, His wisdom, His identity.

RLT, p. 270

As long as we can believe that godhood is an impossible attainment for ourselves, we don't have to push ourselves to higher levels of consciousness and loving activity; we can relax and just be human.

RLT, p. 270

As soon as we believe it is possible for man to become God, we can really never rest for long. We must constantly push ourselves to greater and greater wisdom, greater and greater effectiveness.

RLT, p. 270–271

The fact that God is actively nurturing us so that we might grow up to be like Him brings us face to face with our own laziness.

RLT, p. 271

If we overcome laziness, all the other impediments to spiritual growth will be overcome. If we do not, none of the others will be hurdled.

RLT, p. 271

In debating the wisdom of a proposed course of action, human beings routinely fail to obtain God's side of the issue.

RLT, p. 273

If we seriously listen to the "God within us," we usually find ourselves being urged to take the more difficult path, the path of more effort rather than less. Each and every one of us will hold back and seek to avoid this painful step.

RLT, p. 273

The basis of the fear of change is laziness; it is the fear of the work we would have to do.

RLT, p. 274

To question God may let us in for a lot of work. But a moral of the story [of Adam and Eve] is that it must be done.

RLT, p. 274

Our personal involvement in the fight against evil in the world is one of the ways we grow.

RLT, p. 279

A mark of the spiritually advanced is their awareness of their own laziness.

RLT, p. 280

Lf you want to know the
closest place to look for grace, it is
within yourself.

RLT, p. 281

If you desire wisdom greater than your own, you can find it inside you.

RLT, p. 281

To put it plainly, our un-conscious is God. God within us. God has been with us all along, is now, and always will be.

RLT, p. 281

In my vision the collective unconscious is God; the conscious is man as individual; and the personal unconscious is the interface between them. And the point of spiritual growth is to become God while preserving consciousness.

RLT, p. 282–283

It is because our conscious self resists our unconscious wisdom that we become ill.

RLT, p. 282

We are born that we might become, as a conscious individual, a new life form of God.

RLT, p. 283

The goal of theology and that of most mystics is not to become an egoless, unconscious babe. Rather it is to develop a mature, conscious ego which then can become the ego of God.

RLT, p. 283

If we can identify our mature free will with that of God, we will then have become one form of the grace of God, working on His behalf among mankind, creating love where love did not exist before, and pushing the plane of human evolution forward.

RLT, p. 283–284

Political power is the capacity to coerce others to do one's will. Spiritual power is the capacity to make decisions with maximum awareness. It is consciousness.

RLT, p. 284–285

We are often most in the dark when we are the most certain, and the most enlightened when we are the most confused.

RLT, p. 285

Greater awareness does not come in a single blinding flash of enlightenment. It comes slowly, piece by piece, and each piece must be worked for by the patient effort of study and observation of everything, including ourselves.

RLT, p. 285

If the path of spiritual growth is followed long and earnestly enough, gradually we can come to the place where we actually know what we are doing. We can come to power.

RLT, p. 285–286

Those who have grown the most spiritually are those who are the experts in living. For when we truly know what we are doing, we are participating in the omniscience of God.

RLT, p. 286

Invariably when asked the source of their knowledge and power, the truly powerful will reply: "It is not my power. What little power I have is but a minute expression of a far greater power,..." that is all mankind's, all life's, God's.

RLT, p. 286

Aware of their intimate connectedness to God, the truly powerful experience a loss of self which brings with it always a kind of calm ecstasy, a surcease of loneliness, a communication.

RLT, p. 286–287

Joyful though it is, the experience of spiritual power is also terrifying. For the greater one's awareness, the more difficult it is to take action.

RLT, p. 287

We are all generals. Whatever action we take may influence the course of civilization.

RLT, p. 287

The closer one comes to godhood, the more one feels sympathy for God. To participate in God's omniscience is also to share His agony.

RLT, p. 287

Presidents and kings will have their cronies. But the person who has evolved to the highest level of spiritual power will likely have no one with whom to share such depth of understanding. Others may advise, but the decisions are yours alone.

RLT, p. 288

The aloneness of the journey of spiritual growth is a great burden. But in the communion of growing consciousness, of knowing with God, there is enough joy to sustain us.

RLT, p. 288–289

Love is the will to extend oneself for spiritual growth.

RLT, p. 299

People's capacity to love, and hence their will to grow, is nurtured throughout their lives by grace, or God's love.

RLT, p. 300

Grace is available to everyone. We are all cloaked in the love of God, no one less nobly than another.

RLT, p. 300

The call to grace is a promotion, a call to a position of higher responsibility and power.

RLT, p. 301

To be aware of grace, to personally experience its constant presence, to know one's nearness to God, is to know and continually experience an inner tranquility and peace that few possess.

RLT, p. 301

To experience one's closeness to God is also to experience the obligation to be God, to live a life of service and whatever sacrifice seems required.

RLT, p. 301

Most of us believe that the freedom and power of adulthood is our due, but we have little taste for adult responsibility and self-discipline.

RLT, p. 304

To rise to a position of such power that we have no one to blame except ourselves is a fearful state of affairs. Were it not for God's presence with us in that exalted position, we would be terrified by our aloneness.

RLT, p. 304

Most people want peace without the aloneness of power. And they want the self-confidence of adulthood without having to grow up.

RLT, p. 304

We are accustomed to imagining the experience of the sudden call to grace as an "Oh joy!" phenomenon. In my experience, more often than not it is an "Oh, shit" phenomenon.

RLT, p. 305

At the moment we finally listen to the call to grace we may say, "Oh, thank you, Lord"; or we may say, "O Lord, I am not worthy"; or we may say, "O Lord, do I have to?"

RLT, p. 305

We do not come to grace; grace comes to us.

RLT, p. 306

While on one level we do choose whether or not to heed the call of grace, on another it seems clear that God is the one who does the choosing.

RLT, p. 307

If we can make ourselves into totally disciplined, wholly loving individuals, then, even though we may be ignorant of theology and give no thought to God, we will have prepared ourselves well for the coming of grace.

RLT, p. 307

While we cannot will ourselves to grace, we can by will open ourselves to its miraculous coming.

RLT, p. 307

It is through the paradoxical mixture of seeking and not seeking that we obtain the gift of serendipity and the blessings of grace.

RLT, p. 308

Everyone wants to be loved. But first we must make ourselves lovable by becoming loving, disciplined human beings.

RLT, p. 309

When we nurture ourselves and others without a primary concern of finding reward, then we will have become lovable, and the reward of being loved, which we have not sought, will find us.

RLT, p. 309

With the learned capacity to recognize the gifts of grace, we will find that our journey is guided by the invisible hand and unimaginable wisdom of God with infinitely greater accuracy than that of which our unaided conscious will is capable.

RLT, p. 309

While the words of the prophets and the assistance of grace are available, the journey must still be traveled alone.

RLT, p. 310

Rituals are only learning aids, they are not the learning— eating organic food, saying five Hail Mary's before breakfast, praying facing east or west, or going to church on Sunday will not take you to your destination.

RLT, p. 310

The existence of grace is evidence not only of the reality of God but also of the reality that God's will is devoted to the growth of the individual human spirit.

RLT, p. 311

Through grace we are helped not to stumble and through grace we know that we are being welcomed to the Kingdom of God. What more can we ask?

RLT, p. 311

The human race is in the midst of making an evolutionary leap. "Whether or not we succeed in that leap is your personal responsibility."

RLT, p. 311

It is clearly no longer enough to be simply social animals. Our essential, central, crucial task is to transform ourselves into community creatures. It is the only way that human evolution will be able to proceed.

DD, p. 165

Be fully aware of human variety, and you will recognize the interdependence of humanity.

DD, p. 65

In becoming fully human, we are called to be individuals. We are called to be unique and different. We are called to power.

DD, p. 54

We must attempt, as best as we can, to be captains of our own ships if not exactly masters of our destiny.

DD, p. 54

As women, we need to strengthen our masculine sides; as men, our feminine sides. If we are to grow, we must work on the weak spots that prevent growth.

DD, p. 54

We can never be completely whole in and of ourselves. We are inevitably social creatures who desperately need each other not merely for sustenance, not merely for company, but for any meaning to our lives whatsoever.

DD, p. 54–55

When a group of monks asked a rabbi for advice on saving their dying order, he responded, "I am sorry. The only thing I can tell you is that the Messiah is one of you." Pondering this, the old monks began to treat each other, and themselves, with extraordinary respect on the off chance that one among them might be the Messiah.

DD, p. 14–15

I am dubious as to how far we can move toward global community—which is the only way to achieve international peace—until we learn the basic principles of community in our own individual lives and personal spheres of influence.

DD, p. 17–18

It is not impractical to consider seriously changing the rules of the game when the game is clearly killing you.

DD, p. 18

If humankind is to survive,
the matter of changing the rules is
not optional.

DD, p. 19

Spiritual healing is a process of becoming whole or holy, of becoming increasingly conscious.

DD, p. 19

Perhaps the most extraordinary result of nuclear technology is that it has brought the human race as a whole to the point at which physical and spiritual salvation are no longer separable.

DD, p. 19

It is no longer possible for us to save our skins while remaining ignorant of our own motives and unconscious of our own cultures.

DD, p. 19

We cannot save our skins without saving our souls. We cannot heal the mess we have made of the world without undergoing some kind of spiritual healing.

DD, p. 19

Community, which includes all faiths and all cultures without obliterating them, is the cure for "the core of our greatest contemporary trouble."

DD, p. 20

"Freedom" and "love" are simple words. They are not simple actions.

DD, p. 21

The proper radical is one who tries to get to the root of things, not to be distracted by superficials, to see the woods for the trees. Anyone who thinks *deeply* will be one.

DD, p. 25

Genuine love consistently requires some very hard decisions.

DD, p. 21

Full healing is a lengthy journey. At fifty I am still completing the process of learning how to ask for help, how not to be afraid to appear weak when I am weak, how to allow myself to be dependent and unself-reliant when appropriate.

DD, p. 28

All our enemies are relatives [as in a stressful family that we are necessarily and realistically dependent upon] and all of us play roles for each other in the order of things.

DD, p. 35

Simply seek happiness, and you are not likely to find it. Seek to create and love without regard to your happiness, and you will likely be happy much of the time.

DD, p. 40

Seeking joy in and of itself will not bring it to you. Do the work of creating community, and you will obtain it.

DD, p. 40

Many of both the strongest and weakest of us are indeed crippled heroes.

DD, p. 45

We cannot be truly ourselves until we are able to share freely the things we most have in common: our weakness, our incompleteness, our imperfection, our inadequacy, our sins, our lack of wholeness and self-sufficiency.

DD, p. 58

Ever since knowing that a group of very different people loving one another was potentially repeatable, I have never been able to feel totally hopeless about the human condition.

DD, p. 52

We are called to wholeness and simultaneously to recognize our incompleteness; called to power *and* to acknowledge our weakness; called to both individuation *and* interdependence.

DD, p. 56

Community, like marriage, requires that we hang in there when the going gets a little rough.

DD, p. 62

In community, instead of being ignored, denied, hidden, or changed, human differences are celebrated as gifts.

DD, p. 62

Incorporating the dark and the light, the sacred and the profane, the sorrow and the joy, the glory and the mud, the conclusions of a community are more well rounded than those of an individual, couple, or ordinary group.

DD, p. 65

Begin to appreciate each other's gifts, and you begin to appreciate your own limitations.

DD, p. 65

Witness others share their brokenness, and you will become able to accept your own inadequacy and imperfection.

DD, p. 65

Self-examination is the key to insight, which is the key to wisdom.

DD, p. 66

As the members of a community become vulnerable and find themselves being valued and appreciated, the walls come tumbling down, the love and acceptance escalates, and the healing and converting begins.

DD, p. 68

Community is a safe place precisely because no one is attempting to heal or convert you, to fix you, to change you. Instead, the members accept you as you are.

DD, p. 68

When we are safe, there
is a natural tendency for us to heal
and convert ourselves.

DD, p. 68

As the masks of our composure drop and we see the suffering and courage and brokenness and deeper dignity underneath, we truly start to respect each other as fellow human beings.

DD, p. 69

The reality is that every human being is broken and vulnerable. How strange that we should ordinarily feel compelled to hide our wounds when we are all wounded!

DD, p. 69

There is pain in our wounds. But even more important is the love that arises among us when we share, both ways, our woundedness.

DD, p. 70

Spirit is slippery. It does not submit itself to definition, to capture, the way material things do.

DD, p. 74

We are all in need, in crisis, although most of us still seek to hide the reality of our brokenness from ourselves and one another.

DD. p. 78

The Chinese word for crisis consists of two characters: one represents "danger" and the other "hidden opportunity."

DD, p. 79

The healthy life is hardly one marked by an absence of crises. In fact, an individual's psychological health is distinguished by how *early* he or she can meet crisis.

DD, p. 79

We do not have to manufacture crises in our lives; we have merely to recognize that they exist.

DD, p. 80

Perhaps miracles simply obey laws that we humans generally and currently do not understand.

DD, p. 83

Fighting is far better than
pretending you are not divided.

DD, p. 94

Until such time as we can empty ourselves of expectations and stop trying to fit others and our relationships with them into a pre-conceived mold we cannot really listen, hear, or experience.

DD, p. 95

"Life is what happens when you've planned something else."

DD, p. 95

Often the most loving thing we can do when a friend is in pain is to *share* the pain—to be there even when we have nothing to offer except our presence and even when being there is painful to ourselves.

DD, p. 97

We must be willing to fail and to appreciate the truth that often "Life is not a problem to be solved but a mystery to be lived."

DD, p. 99

OCTOBER 2

Sacrifice hurts because it is a kind of death, the kind of death that is necessary for rebirth.

DD, p. 100

In order to truly listen we have to *truly* empty ourselves, even of our distaste for expressions of pain and suffering.

DD, p. 101

We must embrace not only the light of life but also life's darkness.

DD, p. 102

Going into the unknown is invariably frightening, but we learn what is significantly new only through adventures.

DD, p. 107

We cannot, by ourselves, heal or convert. But if we can empty ourselves of our desires to fix people, healing and converting will effortlessly begin.

DD, p. 113

People would generally much rather depend upon a leader to tell them what to do than determine that for themselves.

DD, p. 115

M

embers who speak
not a word may contribute as much
to a group as the most voluble.

DD, p. 127

It is often painful—sometimes downright traumatic—for people who have effected a change within themselves to reenter a society where nothing has changed.

DD, p. 134

We humans hunger for genuine community and will work hard to maintain it precisely because it is the way to live most fully, most vibrantly.

DD, p. 137

Everyone's a potential minister. Their only choice is whether to be a good minister or a bad one.

DD, p. 151

With no structure there is chaos. With total structure there is no room for emptiness.

DD, p. 159

Given the right conditions, it is indeed possible for small groups of people to live together routinely with love and in the spirit of peace.

DD, p. 169

The first step toward community on a grander scale lies in the acceptance of the fact that we are *not*, nor can we ever be, all the same.

DD, p. 170

Community is a state of being together in which people, instead of hiding behind their defenses, learn to lower them, in which instead of attempting to obliterate their differences, people learn not only to accept them but rejoice in them.

DD, p. 171

Reptilelike, we humans slink close to the ground, mired in the mud of our animal nature and the muck of our cultural prejudices. Yet, like birds, we are also of the spirit, capable of soaring in the heavens, transcending our narrow-mindedness and sinful proclivities. Our task is to come to terms with our dragonhood.

DD, p. 172

We can no longer go back to that unself-conscious state of oneness with the world [i.e., the Garden of Eden] but can find our salvation only by going forward through the rigors of the desert into ever deeper levels of consciousness.

DD, p. 172

The primary false notion—the illusion—of human nature is that people are the same.

DD, p. 173

The dynamics of the spiritual journey are one of the complex features we all have in common, and they provide another example of the simultaneous uniqueness and similarity of human beings.

DD, p. 175

No one can doubt the profound difference between the spirit of maleness and the spirit of femaleness. Yet both men and women must come to terms with the very same psychospiritual issues and climb over the same hurdles on their way to maturity.

DD, p. 175

Our extraordinary capacity for transformation is the most essential characteristic of human nature. It is both the basic cause of war and the basic cure for war.

DD, p. 178

It is the most psychologically and spiritually mature among us who are the least likely to grow old mentally.

DD, p. 181

True adults are those who have learned to continually develop and exercise their capacity for transformation.

DD, p. 181

The more we grow, the greater becomes our capacity to empty ourselves of the old so that the new may enter and we may thereby be transformed.

DD, p. 182

The truth will set you free—but first it will make you damn mad.

DD, p. 184

It is not easy for us to change. But it is possible. And it is our glory as human beings.

DD, p. 184

The key to community is the acceptance—in fact, the celebration—of our individual and cultural differences. It is also the key to world peace.

DD, p. 186

We may not like people because of their flaws or immaturities, but the further we ourselves grow, the more we become able to accept—to love—them, flaws and all.

DD, p. 186

Christ's commandment is not to like one another; it is to *love* one another.

DD, p. 186

Mystics acknowledge the enormity of the unknown, but rather than being frightened by it, they seek to penetrate ever deeper into it that they may understand more—even with the realization that the more they understand, the greater the mystery will become.

DD, p. 192

Much of the art of being a good teacher or healer, consists in staying just one step ahead of your patients or pupils. If you are not ahead, it is unlikely that you will be able to lead them anywhere. But if you are two steps ahead, it is likely that you will lose them.

DD, p. 195

We cannot get to God under our own steam. We must allow God to do the directing.

DD, p. 199

We neither can nor should skip over questioning or doubt in our spiritual development.

DD, p. 200

It is only through the process of questioning that we begin to become even dimly aware that the whole point of life is the development of souls.

DD, p. 200

Once we become aware that we are on a journey—that we are all pilgrims—for the first time we can actually begin to cooperate consciously with God in the process.

DD, p. 200

Out of love and commitment to the whole, virtually all of us are capable of transcending our backgrounds and limitations.

DD, p. 202

The degree to which we can develop world community and thereby save our skins is going to depend primarily on the degree to which we human beings can learn to empty ourselves.

DD, p. 209

The virtue of meditation is that whatever comes into emptiness is beyond our control. And it is only from the unforeseen, unexpected, and new that we learn.

DD, p. 210

True contemplation requires that we stop thinking before we are truly able to think with any originality.

DD, p. 211

The contemplative life style is one rich in reflection, meditation, and prayer. *It is a life style dedicated to maximum awareness.*

DD, p. 211

To survive, a community [like an individual] must repetitively stop whatever it is doing to ask *how* it is doing, to think about where it needs to go, and to be empty to hear the answers.

DD, p. 211–212

The ultimate purpose of emptiness is to make room for the different, the unexpected, the new, the better.

DD, p. 212

We cannot let another person into our hearts or minds unless we empty ourselves. We can truly listen to him or truly hear her only out of emptiness.

DD, p. 212

Without silence there is no music; there is only noise.

DD, p. 212

Unless we empty ourselves of preconceived cultural or intellectual images and expectations, we not only cannot understand the Other, we cannot even listen. Indeed, we cannot even feel empathy.

DD, p. 214

Our love, our sacrifices, are made manifest, more than in any other way through our willingness not to know.

DD, p. 219

The capacity to accept ambiguity and to think paradoxically is both one of the qualities of emptiness and one of the requirements for peacemaking.

DD, p. 220

If the only reason to give up something is to gain something better, then we must ask, "Of what do we have to empty ourselves in order to gain peace?"

DD, p. 225

Openness requires of us vulnerability—the ability, even the willingness, to be wounded.

DD, p. 226

A life lacking the emotional upheavals of depression and despair, fear and anxiety, grief and sadness, anger and the agony of forgiving, confusion and doubt, criticism and rejection, will not only be useless to ourselves, it will be useless to others.

DD, p. 227

We cannot heal without being willing to be hurt.

DD, p. 227

If Jesus, the healer, taught us anything, he taught us that the way to salvation lies through vulnerability.

DD, p. 227

We all have problems, imperfections, neuroses, sins, failures. Our imperfections are among the few things we human beings all have in common.

DD, p. 230–231

It is only among the overtly imperfect that we can find community and only among the overtly imperfect nations of the world that we can find peace.

DD, p. 231

"The greatest gift we can give each other is our own woundedness."

DD, p. 231

There can be no vulnerability without risk; and there can be no community without vulnerability; and there can be no peace—ultimately no life—without community.

DD, p. 233

If you wish to discern either the presence or absence of integrity, you need to ask only one question. What is missing? Has anything been left out?

DD, p. 236

As soon as we think with integrity we will realize that we are all properly stewards and that we cannot with integrity deny our responsibility for stewardship of every part of the whole.

DD, p. 239

The flowers in the garden are not "my" flowers. I do not know how to create a flower; I can merely steward or nurture one.

DD, p. 239

At the root of things,
virtually all truth is paradoxical.

DD, p. 238

Truth in religion is characterized by inclusivity and paradox. Falsity in religion can be detected by its one-sidedness and failure to integrate the whole.

DD, p. 240

As a Christian, I can say the whole reality is that God, paradoxically, resides both inside of us in Her "still small voice" and simultaneously outside of us in all His transcendent and magnificent Otherness.

DD, p. 242–243

Salvation is the effect of both grace and good works in a paradoxical mixture that is sufficiently mysterious to defy any mathematical formulation.

DD, p. 243

Mohammed said: "Trust in God, but tie your camel first."

DD, p. 244

While all forms of think-
ing should be tolerated, some forms
of behavior should not be. In the
end it is behavior that counts.

DD, p. 245

The profession of a religious belief is a lie if it does not significantly determine one's economic, political, and social behavior.

DD, p. 246

Any deep relationship will involve—indeed, require—turmoil.

DD, p. 248

I suspect God is big enough not to be terribly bothered if we damn Him now and then. What really infuriates Him, however, is to be *used*.

DD, p. 248

The overall purpose of human communication is—or should be—reconciliation.

DD, p. 257

Confrontive, even angry communication is sometimes necessary to bring into focus the clear reality of the barriers that separate us before they can be knocked down.

DD, p. 257

The proper task of communication is to create love and harmony among us. It is peacemaking.

DD, p. 258

Peacemaking and reconciliation—community-making—is not just a global matter; it is a matter of concern within any business, any church, any neighborhood, any family.

DD, p. 258

The major obstacle to peacemaking is passivity.

DD, p. 262

Dag Hammarskjöld taught us: "In our era, the road to holiness necessarily passes through the world of action."

DD, p. 264

Treat people as if they are violent madmen long enough, and sure enough, they will become violent madmen.

DD, p. 270

Ilf we are to save ourselves we must learn to submit to humanity—and quickly. And until we accept that as our task, we do not truly want peace—only power.

DD, p. 276

The only way to stop play-
ing psychological games is to stop.

DD, p. 277

In order for us to respect ourselves we must have some dignity and the kind of pride that goes with dignity.

DD, p. 286

Today the times demand of us that we take major risks for peace.

DD, p. 295

To be a true Christian one must live dangerously.

DD, p. 296

Each of us—every soul—is a battleground for a struggle between good and evil.

DD, p. 299

One of the characteristics of a true community is that it is a body that can fight gracefully.

DD, p. 300

We are all confronted with the task of achieving maturity. And nowhere can this task be more effectively accomplished than in community, where all members learn to exercise leadership and combat their own tendency to depend upon an authority figure.

DD, p. 316

As a member of a genuine long-term community once said: "We love one another too much to let anyone get away with anything."

DD, p. 319–320

Peacemaking ultimately must begin at a grass-roots level. It begins with you.

DD, p. 325

Remember that being takes precedence over doing.

DD, p. 327

If you concentrate simply upon making your community beautiful, its beauty will shine forth without your having to do anything at all.

DD, p. 327

Genuine community is inclusive and if you are a wealthy white Democrat, you have the most to learn from the poor, the blacks and Chicanos, and the Republicans. You need their gifts to be whole.

DD, p. 328

We are all called to be peacemakers, whether we like it or not.

DD, p. 329

The keystone of the strategy required to win the war of peacemaking is community, and the weapons can be only those of love.

DD, p. 330

Our task is to sell the world on love.

DD, p. 334